sundance
LITTLE GREEN READERS

Litterbug

Focus: Pollution

D1712010

Meredith Costain

Don't throw litter
on the sidewalk.

Don't throw litter
in the water.

Don't throw litter on the playground.

Don't throw litter in the park.

Don't throw litter
in the woods.

Don't throw litter
on the beach.

Don't be a litterbug!
Throw litter in the trash can!